A
MILEAGE &
MAINTENANCE
LOG BOOK

Created by:
Beth L. Wickstrum

HOMETREES PRESS
Ojai • California

Table of Contents

This Mileage Log Book Belongs To:

Automobile Information

Year: _____   Make/Model: _____

License Plate #: _____

VIN #: _____

Date Purchased: _____

Purchased From: _____

Insurance Company: _____

Insurance Agent: _____

Insurance Phone Number: _____

Oil Change Every: _____ Miles

Size of Gas Tank: _____ Gallons

Fuel Type: _____

Registration Renews in: _____

                                        Month

Foreword

This log is intended to help you track your travel miles, gas purchased, car washes, maintenance types and cost.

Use this log for your business and tax reporting. Keep it in your glove compartment where it will be handy.

Once you have completed your taxes for the year, we recommend that you keep this log with your tax records.

Has this book been helpful to you?

If so, please leave us a review on Amazon!
We appreciate your feedback and strive to make useful products to make your life easier.

Please visit our website:

HomeTreesPress.com

Mileage Log

YEAR	MAKE	MODEL

Date/Time	Miles (Begin)	Miles (End)	Total Miles	Notes
			Total Miles:	

Handy Items to Keep in Your Car for Breakdowns

☑   Jumper Cables

☑   Flashlight

☑   LED Road Flares and/or Emergency Triangles (Reflective Models)

☑   A Multi-Tool

☑   Waterproof Tarp

☑   Wipes/Rags/Towel

☑   Water Bottles

☑   Duct Tape

☑   Snacks that will last a long time

☑   Kitty litter for tire traction

Mileage Log

YEAR		MAKE		MODEL

Date/Time	Miles (Begin)	Miles (End)	Total Miles	Notes
			Total Miles:	

Items to Keep in Your Car for Emergencies

☑   A Good First Aid Kit

☑   A Keychain Escape Tool that
              Can Cut Through Seatbelt Webbing

☑   An Emergency Kit with Essentials
              Usually Stored in a Backpack

Mileage Log

YEAR	MAKE	MODEL

Date/Time	Miles (Begin)	Miles (End)	Total Miles	Notes
Total Miles:				

Items to Keep in Your Car for All Weather Conditions

☑   Ice Scraper

☑   An Umbrella

☑   Windshield Sunscreen

Mileage Log

YEAR	MAKE	MODEL

Date/Time	Miles (Begin)	Miles (End)	Total Miles	Notes
		Total Miles:		

Useful Items for Daily Convenience

- ☑ Cell Phone Chargers
- ☑ Pen and Paper (Notebook)
- ☑ Snacks
- ☑ Hand Sanitizer
- ☑ Reusable Grocery Bags
- ☑ Tissues/Toilet Paper/Wet Wipes

Mileage Log

YEAR	MAKE	MODEL

Date/Time	Miles (Begin)	Miles (End)	Total Miles	Notes
Total Miles:				

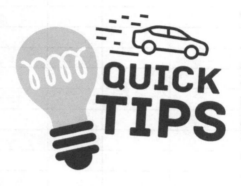

Check your spare tire often and make sure it is inflated.

Mileage Log

YEAR		MAKE		MODEL

Date/Time	Miles (Begin)	Miles (End)	Total Miles	Notes
			Total Miles:	

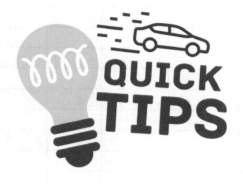

Change the oil according to the
manufacturer's recommendation and
the oil filter.

Mileage Log

YEAR	MAKE	MODEL

Date/Time	Miles (Begin)	Miles (End)	Total Miles	Notes
		Total Miles:		

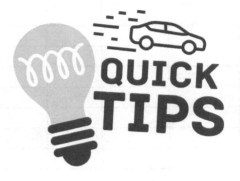

Check your battery for corrosion and keep it clean.

Mileage Log

YEAR	MAKE	MODEL

Date/Time	Miles (Begin)	Miles (End)	Total Miles	Notes
Total Miles:				

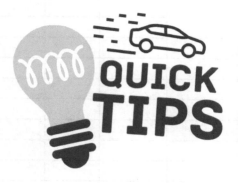

Have your brake pads checked if you hear a squeaking or squealing sound. If your brake fluid is a dark color it needs to be changed.

Mileage Log

YEAR	MAKE	MODEL

Date/Time	Miles (Begin)	Miles (End)	Total Miles	Notes
			Total Miles:	

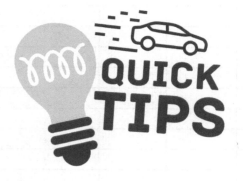

Replace the air filter about every 12,000 miles.

Mileage Log

YEAR	MAKE	MODEL

Date/Time	Miles (Begin)	Miles (End)	Total Miles	Notes
			Total Miles:	

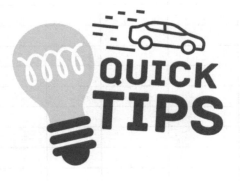

Replace your windshield wipers every 3-6 months.

Mileage Log

YEAR		MAKE		MODEL

Date/Time	Miles (Begin)	Miles (End)	Total Miles	Notes
			Total Miles:	

*Rotate your tires every
5,000 – 7,500 miles.*

Mileage Log

YEAR	MAKE	MODEL

Date/Time	Miles (Begin)	Miles (End)	Total Miles	Notes
Total Miles:				

Check your wheel alignment every 30,000 miles or as recommended and when you install new tires.

Mileage Log

YEAR	MAKE	MODEL

Date/Time	Miles (Begin)	Miles (End)	Total Miles	Notes
			Total Miles:	

*Check the shocks, springs and struts
(suspension system).*

Mileage Log

YEAR	MAKE	MODEL

Date/Time	Miles (Begin)	Miles (End)	Total Miles	Notes
			Total Miles:	

*Check and change out the coolant.
Check your coolant twice a year at
the beginning of the warm weather
season and before winter hits.*

Mileage Log

YEAR		MAKE		MODEL

Date/Time	Miles (Begin)	Miles (End)	Total Miles	Notes
			Total Miles:	

*Check your spark plugs every
30,000 miles.*

Mileage Log

YEAR	MAKE	MODEL

Date/Time	Miles (Begin)	Miles (End)	Total Miles	Notes
		Total Miles:		

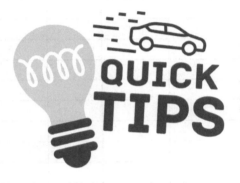

Inspect your belts and hoses.
Be mindful of your belts: An audible
squeaking sound is a good indication
you need to check your belts.

Mileage Log

YEAR		MAKE		MODEL

Date/Time	Miles (Begin)	Miles (End)	Total Miles	Notes
			Total Miles:	

Do an emissions inspection. Replace filters according to the following schedule:

☑   Fuel Filter - every 2 years or 30,000 miles

☑   Engine Air Filter - every 15,000-30,000 miles

☑   Cabin Air Filter - every 15,000-20,000 miles

☑   Emission Filter - every 100,000 miles

Mileage Log

YEAR	MAKE	MODEL

Date/Time	Miles (Begin)	Miles (End)	Total Miles	Notes
			Total Miles:	

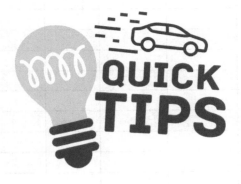

Lighten The Load On Your Keychain –
*the constant swinging back and
forth can wear out the ignition switch.*

Mileage Log

YEAR		MAKE		MODEL

Date/Time	Miles (Begin)	Miles (End)	Total Miles	Notes
			Total Miles:	

Check your tire tread and check that your tires are properly inflated.

Mileage Log

YEAR	MAKE	MODEL

Date/Time	Miles (Begin)	Miles (End)	Total Miles	Notes
		Total Miles:		

*Protect the paint on your car
with a coat of wax.*

Mileage Log

YEAR	MAKE	MODEL

Date/Time	Miles (Begin)	Miles (End)	Total Miles	Notes
		Total Miles:		

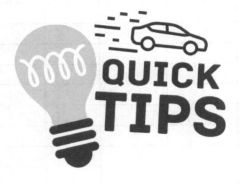

*Prevent moisture from entering
the inside of the car –
You don't want mold!*

Mileage Log

YEAR	MAKE	MODEL

Date/Time	Miles (Begin)	Miles (End)	Total Miles	Notes
		Total Miles:		

Check Your Windshield for Cracks.

Mileage Log

YEAR	MAKE	MODEL

Date/Time	Miles (Begin)	Miles (End)	Total Miles	Notes
			Total Miles:	

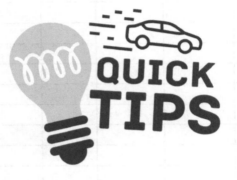

Drive Less Aggressively!

Mileage Log

YEAR	MAKE	MODEL

Date/Time	Miles (Begin)	Miles (End)	Total Miles	Notes
		Total Miles:		

*Practice Weekly Washes –
Protect Your Clear Coat.*

Mileage Log

YEAR	MAKE	MODEL

Date/Time	Miles (Begin)	Miles (End)	Total Miles	Notes
			Total Miles:	

Don't Smoke in the Cabin - this is a fast way to lower your car's value.

Mileage Log

YEAR		MAKE		MODEL

Date/Time	Miles (Begin)	Miles (End)	Total Miles	Notes
			Total Miles:	

Don't race your car's engine when you start it up. Accelerate slowly when you begin your drive. The most wear to the engine and drive train occurs in the first 10 to 20 minutes of operation.

Mileage Log

YEAR	MAKE	MODEL

Date/Time	Miles (Begin)	Miles (End)	Total Miles	Notes
	Total Miles:			

*Do not idle your car in the
driveway thinking you are
warming up the engine.*

Mileage Log

YEAR	MAKE	MODEL

Date/Time	Miles (Begin)	Miles (End)	Total Miles	Notes
Total Miles:				

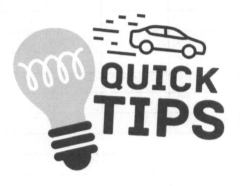

Pay attention to the weather.
Avoid accelerating quickly or driving at
high speeds and accelerating
rapidly when it is very
hot or cold outside

Mileage Log

YEAR	MAKE	MODEL

Date/Time	Miles (Begin)	Miles (End)	Total Miles	Notes
		Total Miles:		

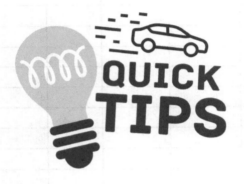

Being a safe, careful driver will extend the life of your tires.

Mileage Log

YEAR	MAKE	MODEL

Date/Time	Miles (Begin)	Miles (End)	Total Miles	Notes
Total Miles:				

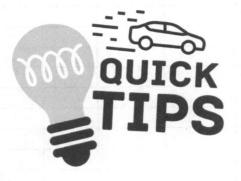

*Try to consolidate your
short driving trips.*

Gas Usage Log

YEAR	MAKE	MODEL

Date	Price per Gallon	Total Gallons	Gas Cost
		Total Gas Cost:	

Gas Usage Log

YEAR	MAKE	MODEL

Date	Price per Gallon	Total Gallons	Gas Cost
		Total Gas Cost:	

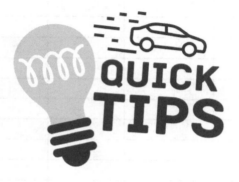

Don't fill up if you see a gasoline tanker truck at the gas station. The sediment stirred up when the fuel tanks are being filled can clog your filters and fuel injectors.

Gas Usage Log

YEAR	MAKE	MODEL

Date	Price per Gallon	Total Gallons	Gas Cost
		Total Gas Cost:	

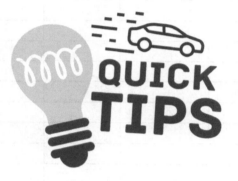

*Only buy gas at reputable
gas stations.*

Gas Usage Log

YEAR	MAKE	MODEL

Date	Price per Gallon	Total Gallons	Gas Cost
	Total Gas Cost:		

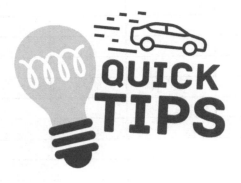

Safety Tip: Use the Dutch Reach Open your door with your RIGHT hand. This will force you to look over your left shoulder for bikers and other cars.

Gas Usage Log

YEAR	MAKE	MODEL

Date	Price per Gallon	Total Gallons	Gas Cost
	Total Gas Cost:		

Gas Usage Log

YEAR	MAKE	MODEL

Date	Price per Gallon	Total Gallons	Gas Cost
		Total Gas Cost:	

Park in the shade to minimize the sun's impact on the interior and exterior of your car.

Oil Change/Lube/Tire Rotation Log

YEAR	MAKE	MODEL

Date	Oil Change/Lube	Tire Rotation	Cost
		Total Cost:	

Always be a defensive driver.

Oil Change/Lube/Tire Rotation Log

YEAR	MAKE	MODEL

Date	Oil Change/Lube	Tire Rotation	Cost
		Total Cost:	

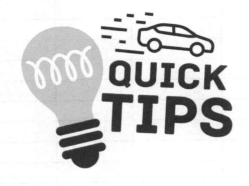

Do NOT Tailgate. Drive smoothly.

Auto Maintenance Log

YEAR	MAKE	MODEL

Date	Maintenance Type	Cost
	Total Cost:	

Auto Maintenance Log

YEAR	MAKE	MODEL

Date	Maintenance Type	Cost
	Total Cost:	

Take it easy if your tires get stuck.
Use a traction aid like
sand or kitty litter.

Car Wash Log

YEAR	MAKE	MODEL

Date	Cost	Tip	Total
Total Cost for Car Washes:			

Car Wash Log

YEAR	MAKE	MODEL

Date	Cost	Tip	Total
Total Cost for Car Washes:			

Car Wash Log

YEAR	MAKE	MODEL

Date	Cost	Tip	Total
Total Cost for Car Washes:			

How should a passenger open the passenger door?

With their left hand!

Reach - Swivel - Look - Open

Notes

Notes

Notes

Notes

Notes

Notes

Notes

Made in United States
Troutdale, OR
03/04/2024

18190730R00060